Black History in Columbus GA

A coloring book featuring some of the many local landmarks

of Columbus Ga that are a part of the rich Black history of the area.

Table of Contents

1. The Columbus Black History Museum and Archives - Located at 315 8th Street, the museum is volunteer run and a great place to learn more about the locations featured in this coloring book.
2. The old St John AME building located at 1510 5th Avenue, ST John is the second AME church in Columbus, established in 1870.
3. The Dillingham Street Bridge crosses the Chattahoochee river between Columbus, GA and Phoenix City, AL. As a slave and as a free man Master Bridge Builder Horace King worked on the bridge during his lifetime.
4. St James AME located at 1002 6th Ave is the oldest AME congregation in Georgia.
5. Fifth Avenue School located at 627 5th Avenue was built in 1908 and provided grades 5 through 9.
6. First African Baptist Church located at 901 5th Ave was founded in 1830 has the distinction of being the oldest black church in Columbus.
7. The Spencer House located at 745 Veterans Parkway was built in 1912 and was home to William H Spencer. Mr Spencer was the first black person to serve as "Supervisor of Colored Schools" in Muscogee County.
8. Holsey Chapel CME Church located at 718 8th St was established in 1884.
9. City Mills and Dam located at 1st Avenue and 18th St built by Horace King.
10. Greater Shady Grove Missionary Baptist Church located at 1901 2nd Ave was established in 1863 in an oak grove.
11. Mildred L Terry Library located at 640 Veterans Parkway was built during the 1950s to service the black community during segregation.
12. Fourth Street Missionary Baptist Church located at 222 5th St. Grew out of the Mt Canaan Baptist church established in 1900.
13. The Claflin School located at 1532 5th Ave, the first school in Columbus for black students was built by the Freedmen's Bureau after the Civil War. The current school was built in 1920.
14. Metropolitan Baptist Church located at 1633 5th Ave. Established in 1890 as an outgrowth from First African Baptist, hosts "Emancipation Day" celebration annually.
15. Friendship Baptist Church located at 831 6th Ave. Established in 1892, Ma Rainey was a member and sang in the choir.
16. Ma Rainey Home located at 805 5th Avenue. The home of Blues legend Ma Rainey after her retirement.
17. St John AME 3980 Steam Mill Road. After major damage by tornado in 1990 the congregation moved to the present location.

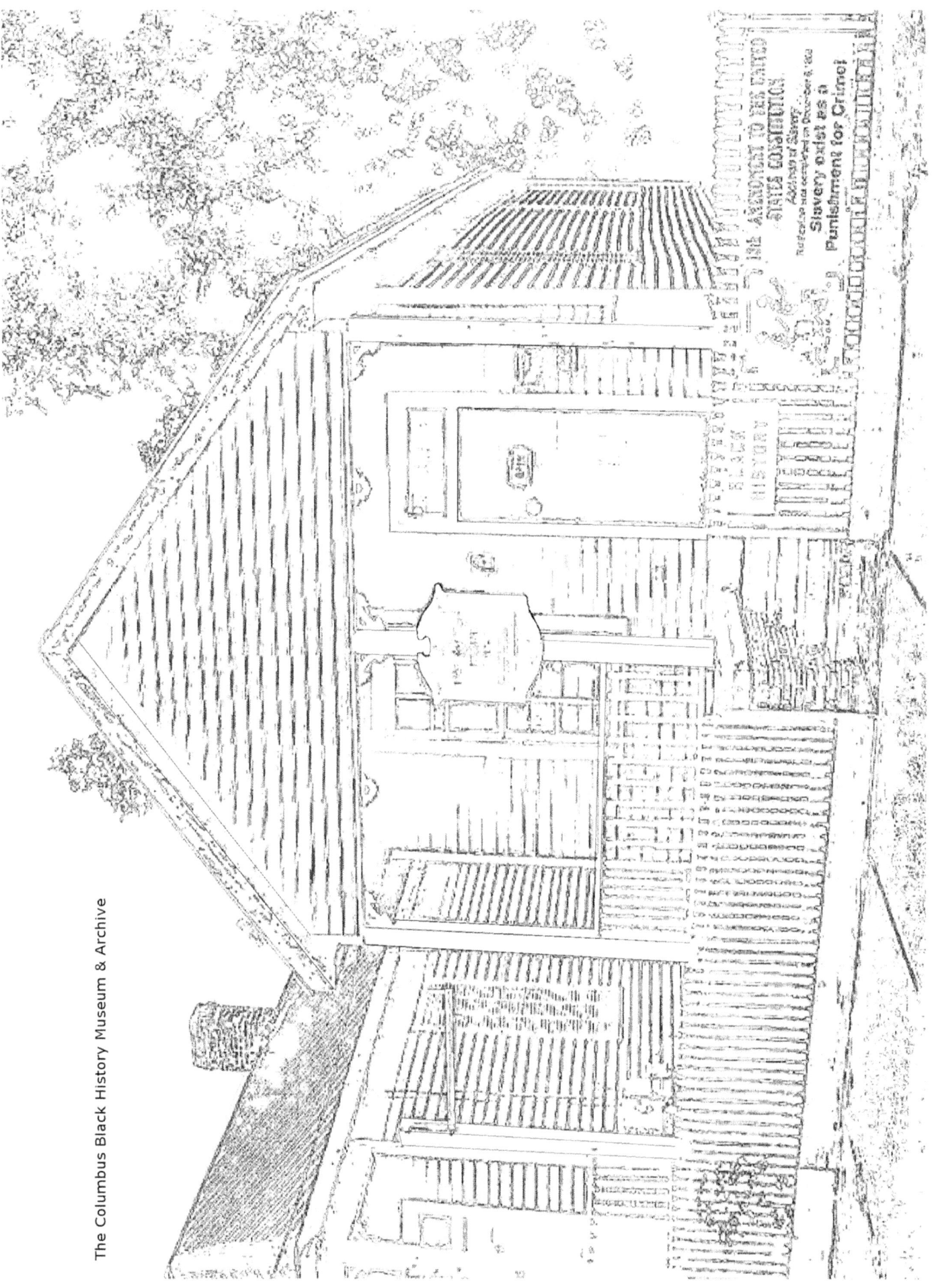

The Columbus Black History Museum & Archive

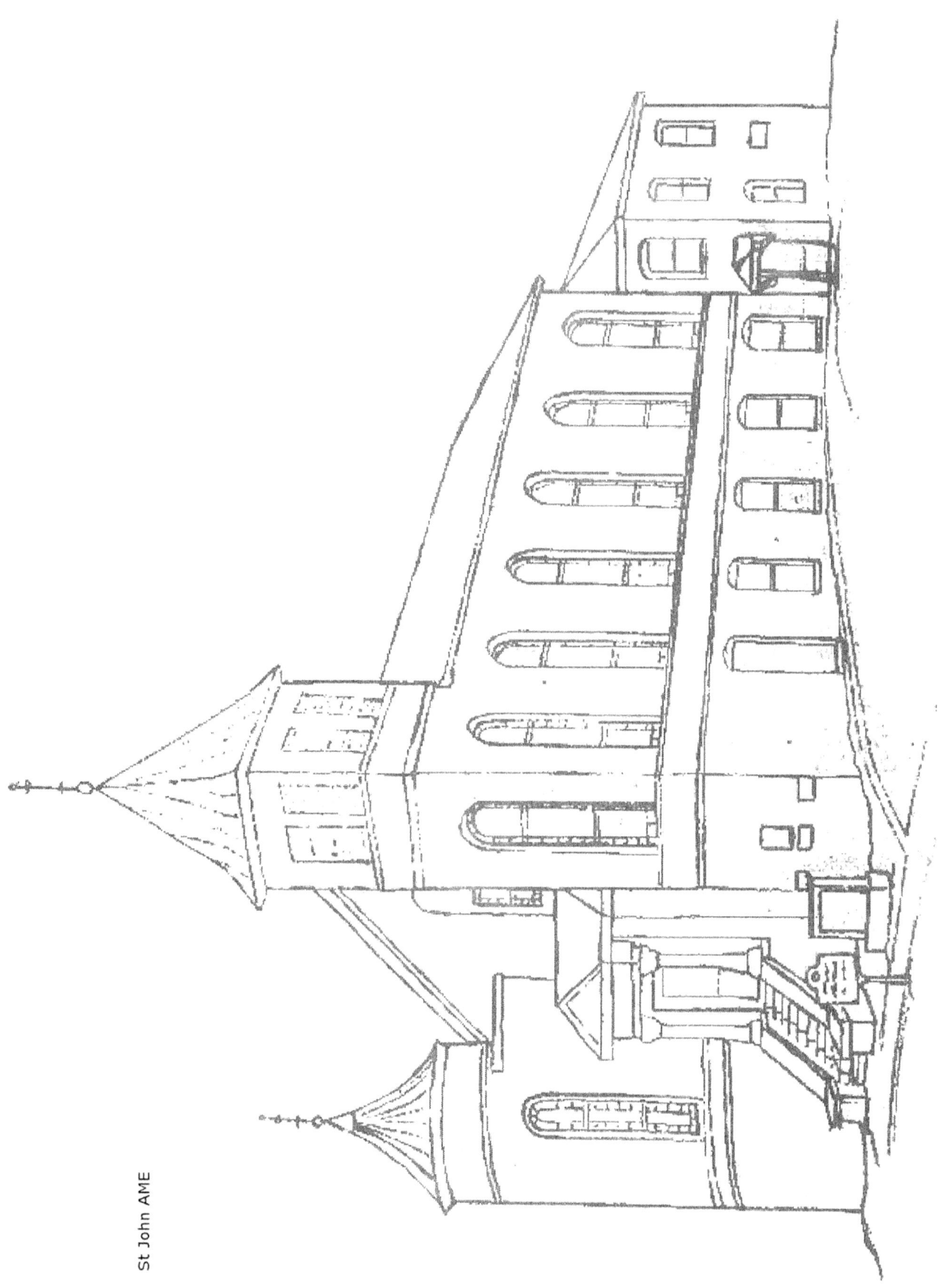

St John AME

The Dillingham Street Bridge

St James AME

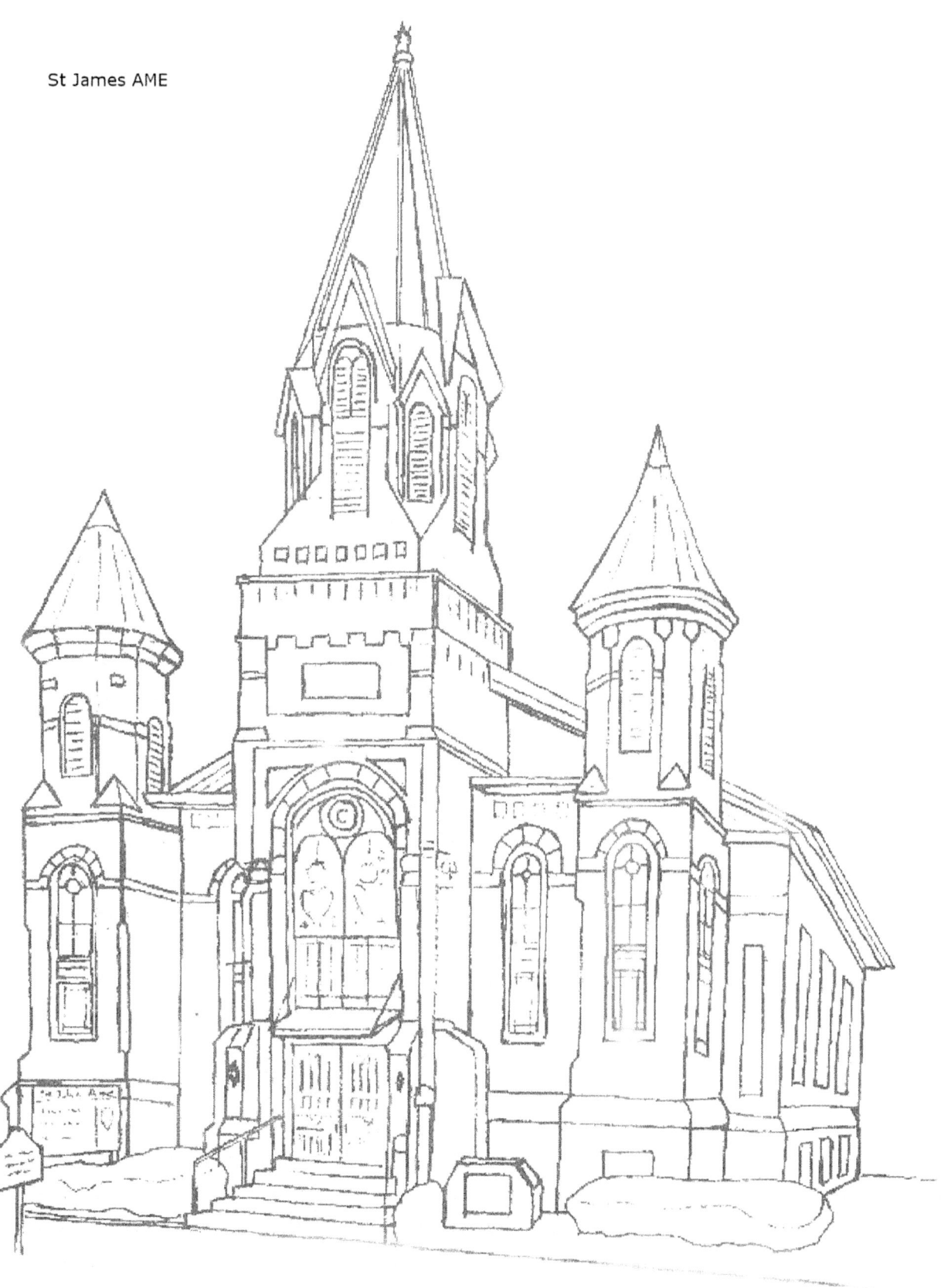

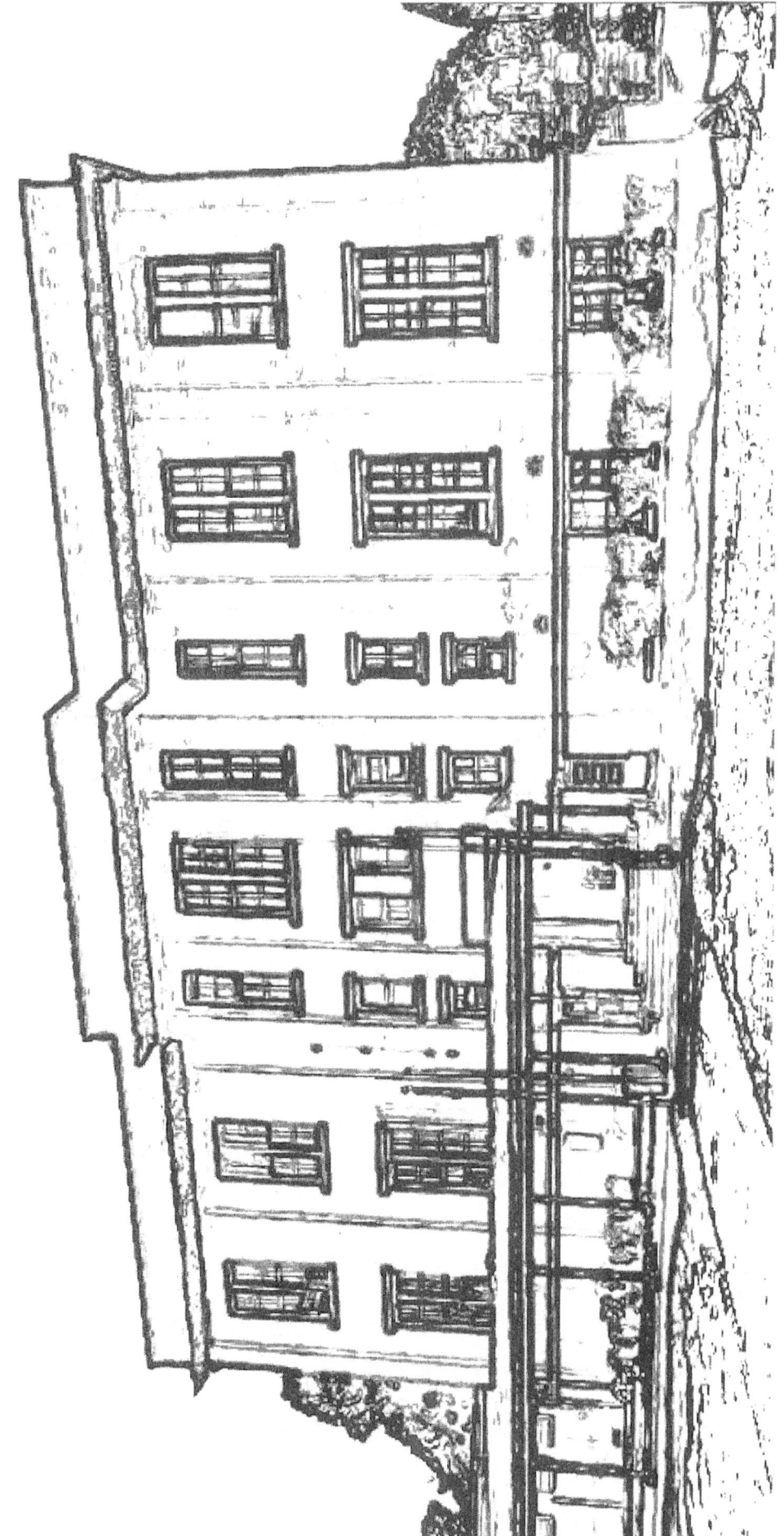

Fifth Avenue School

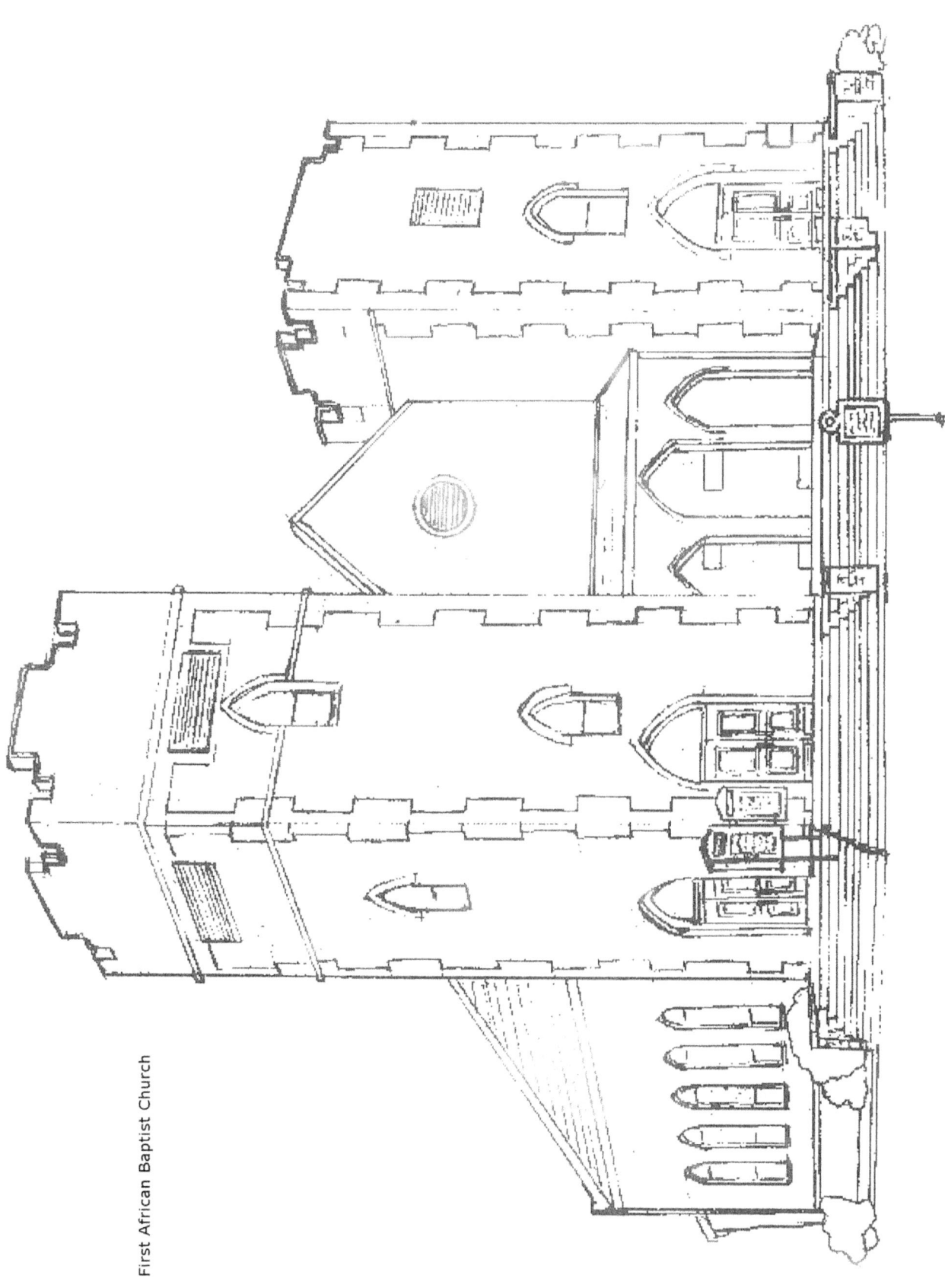

First African Baptist Church

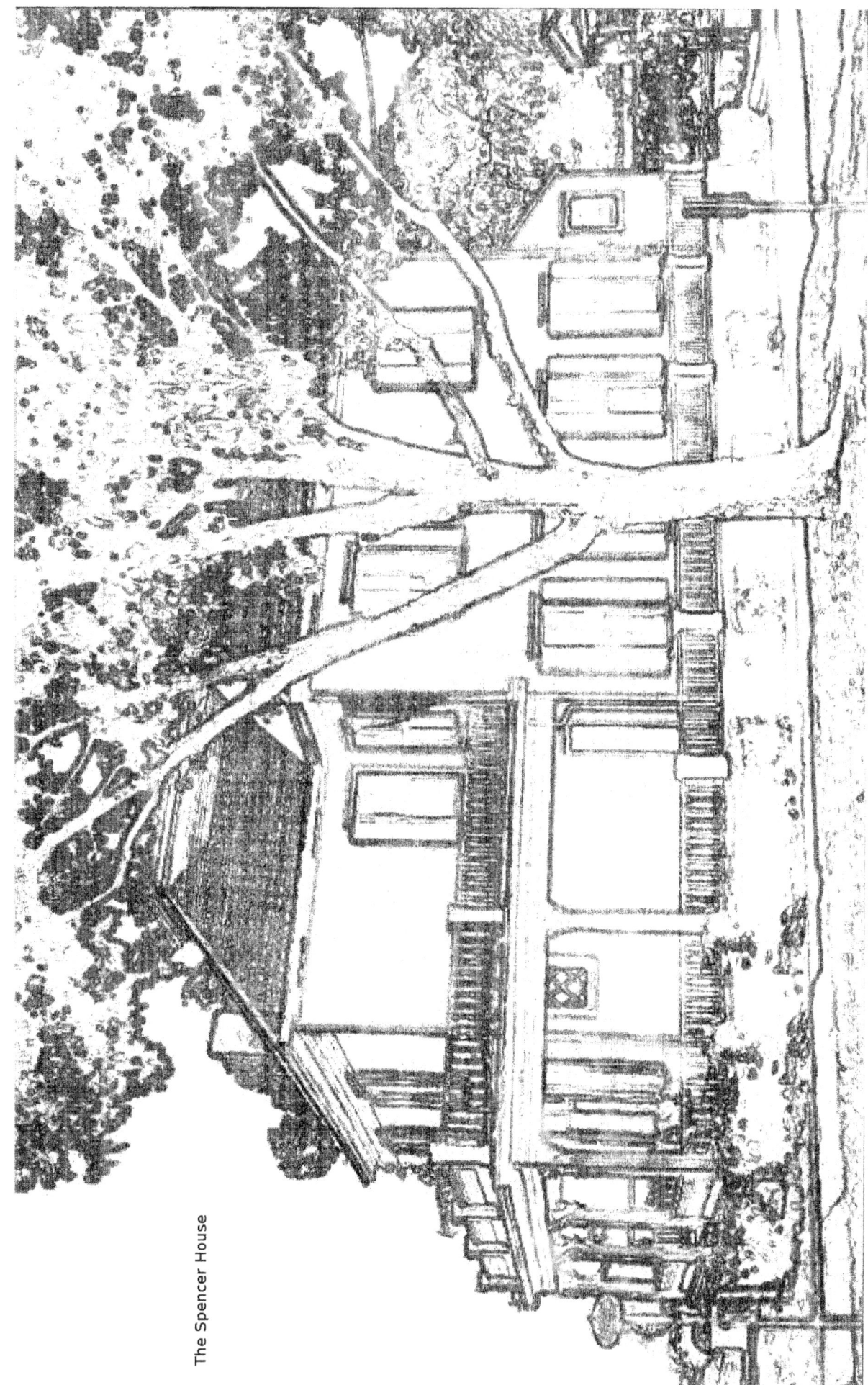

The Spencer House

Holsey Chapel CME

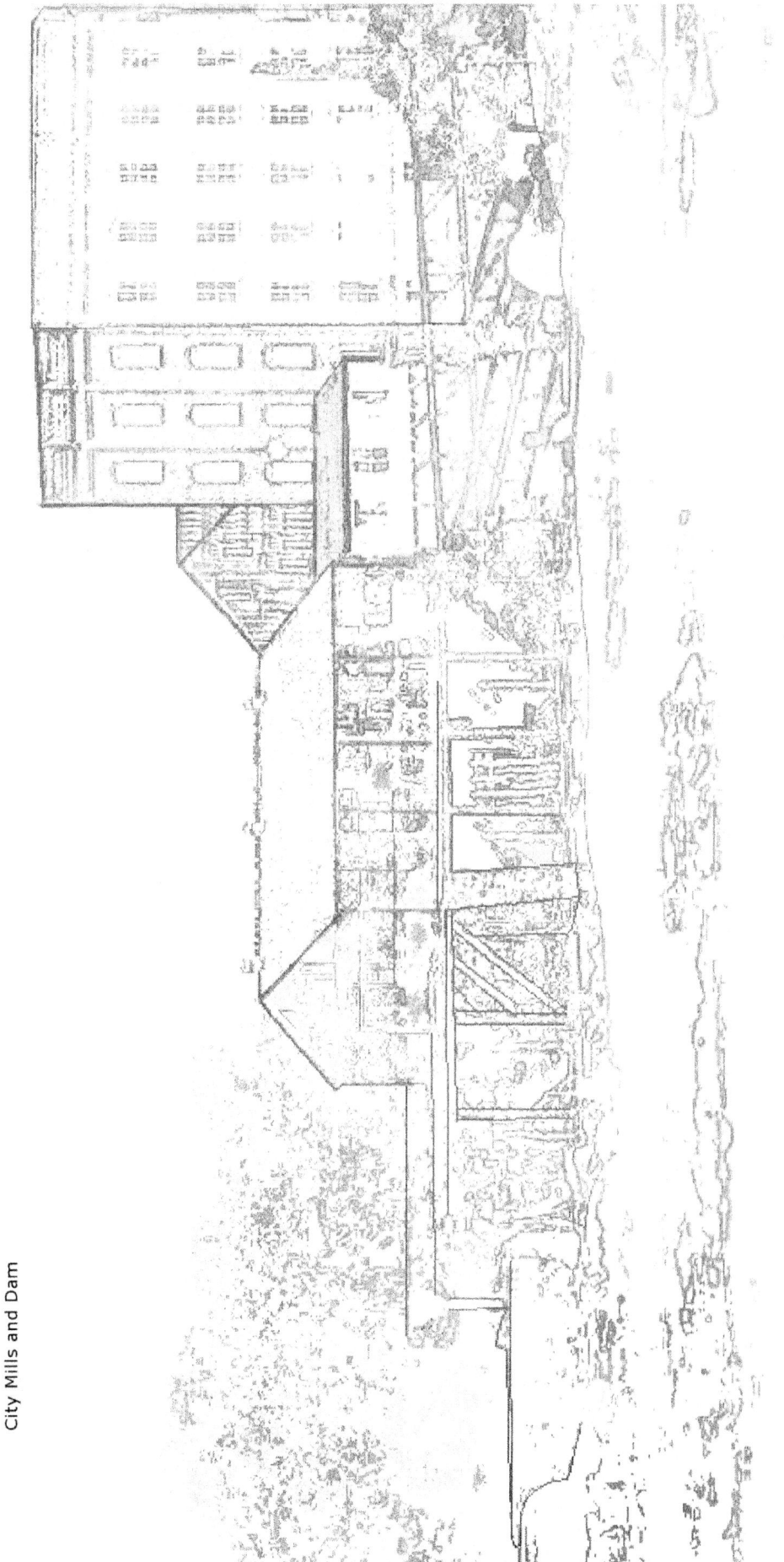

City Mills and Dam

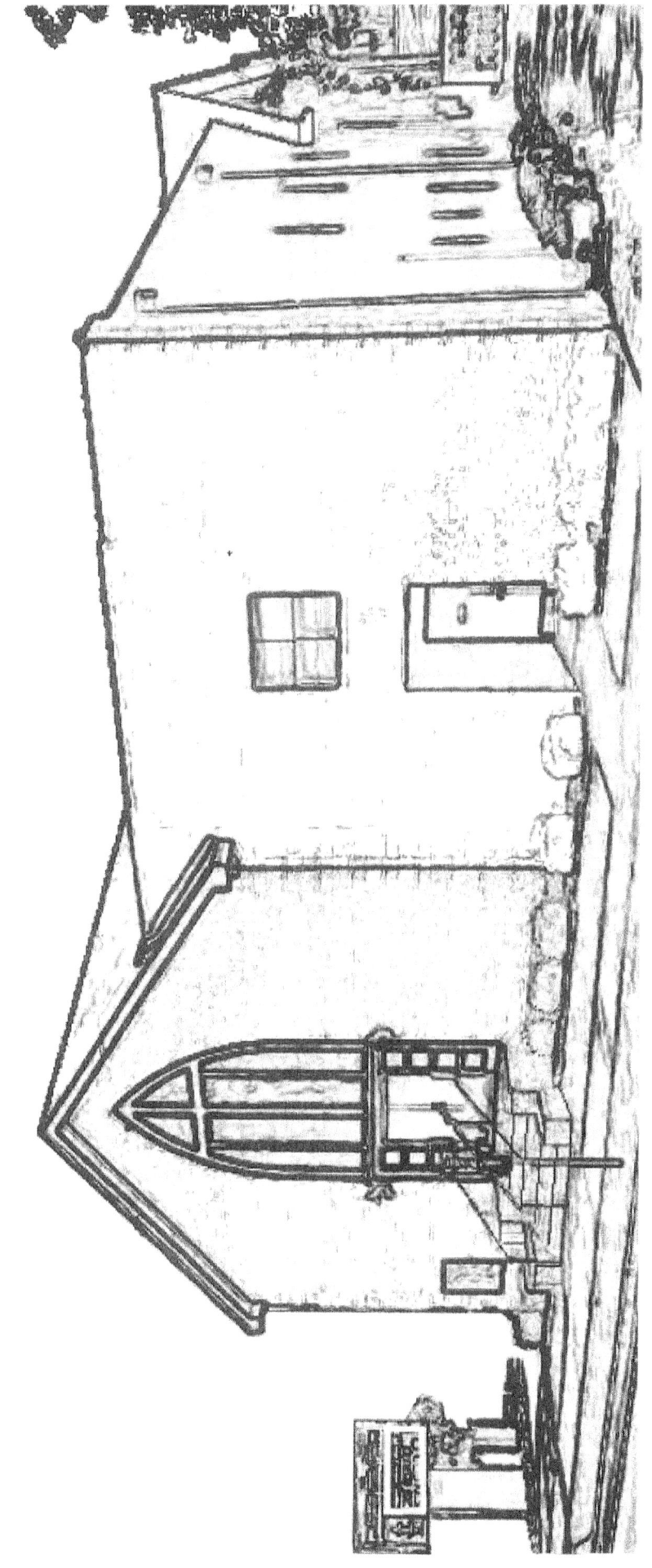

Greater Shady Grove Missionary Baptist Church

The Mildred L Terry Library

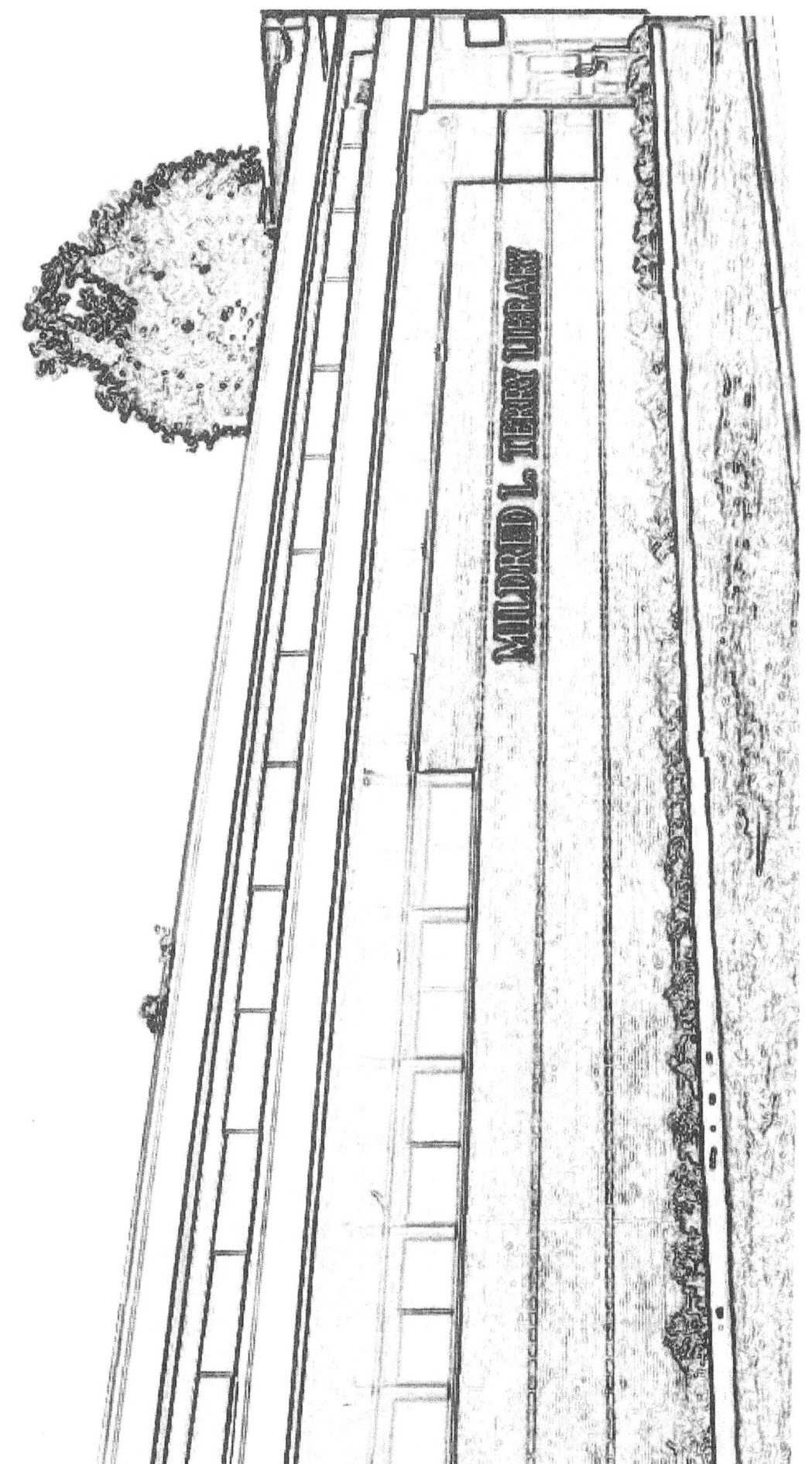

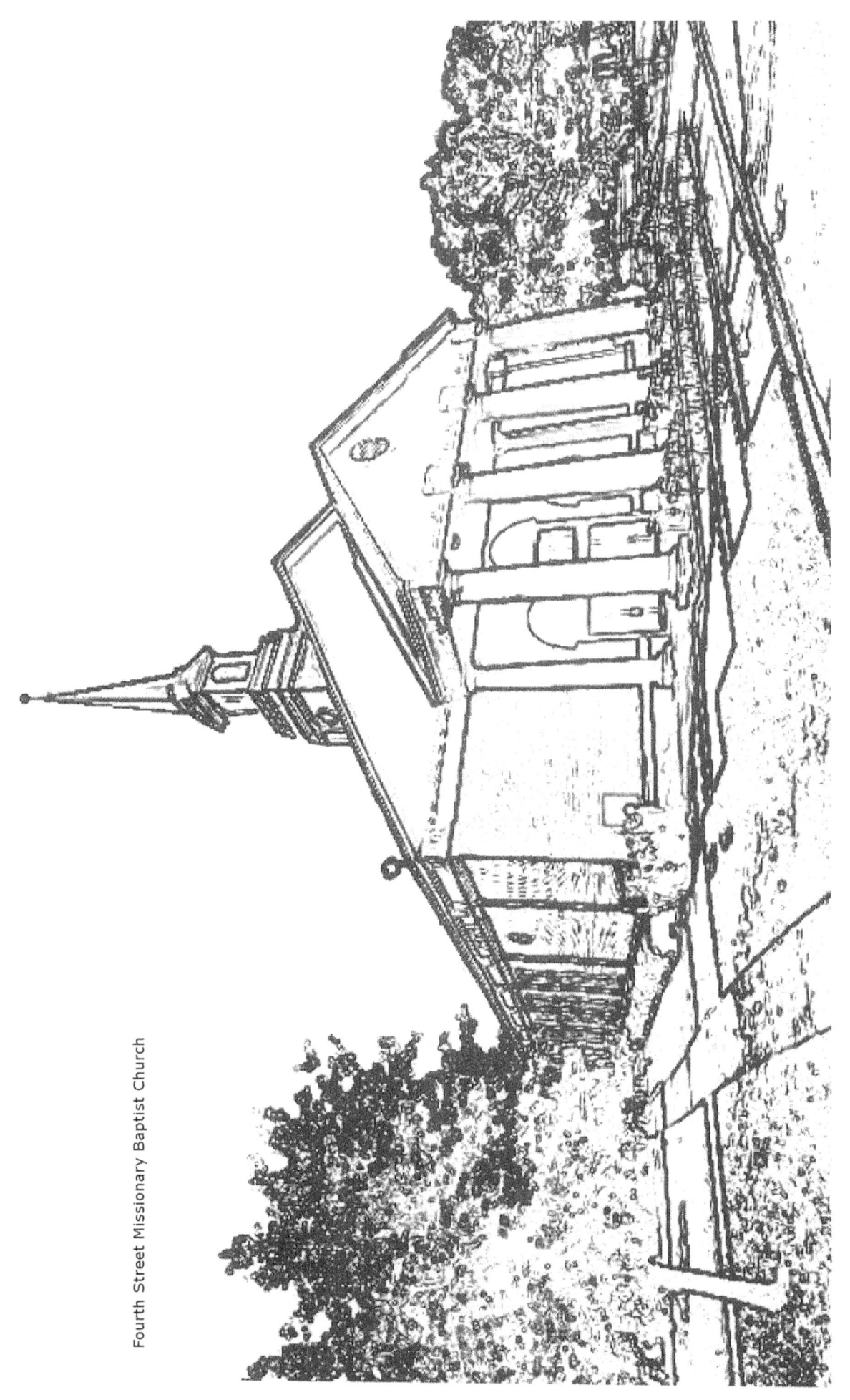

Fourth Street Missionary Baptist Church

The Claflin School

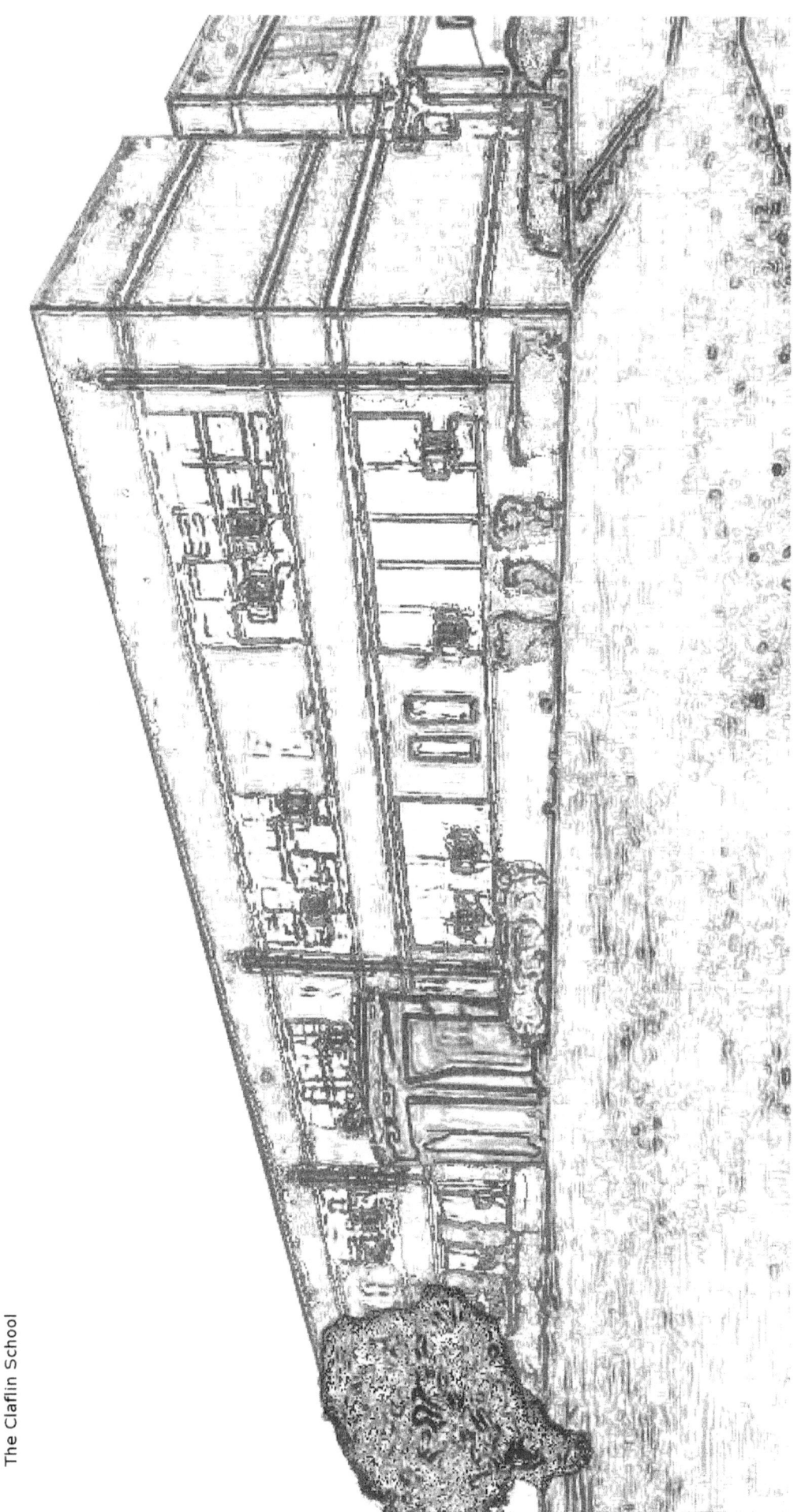

Metropolitan Baptist Church

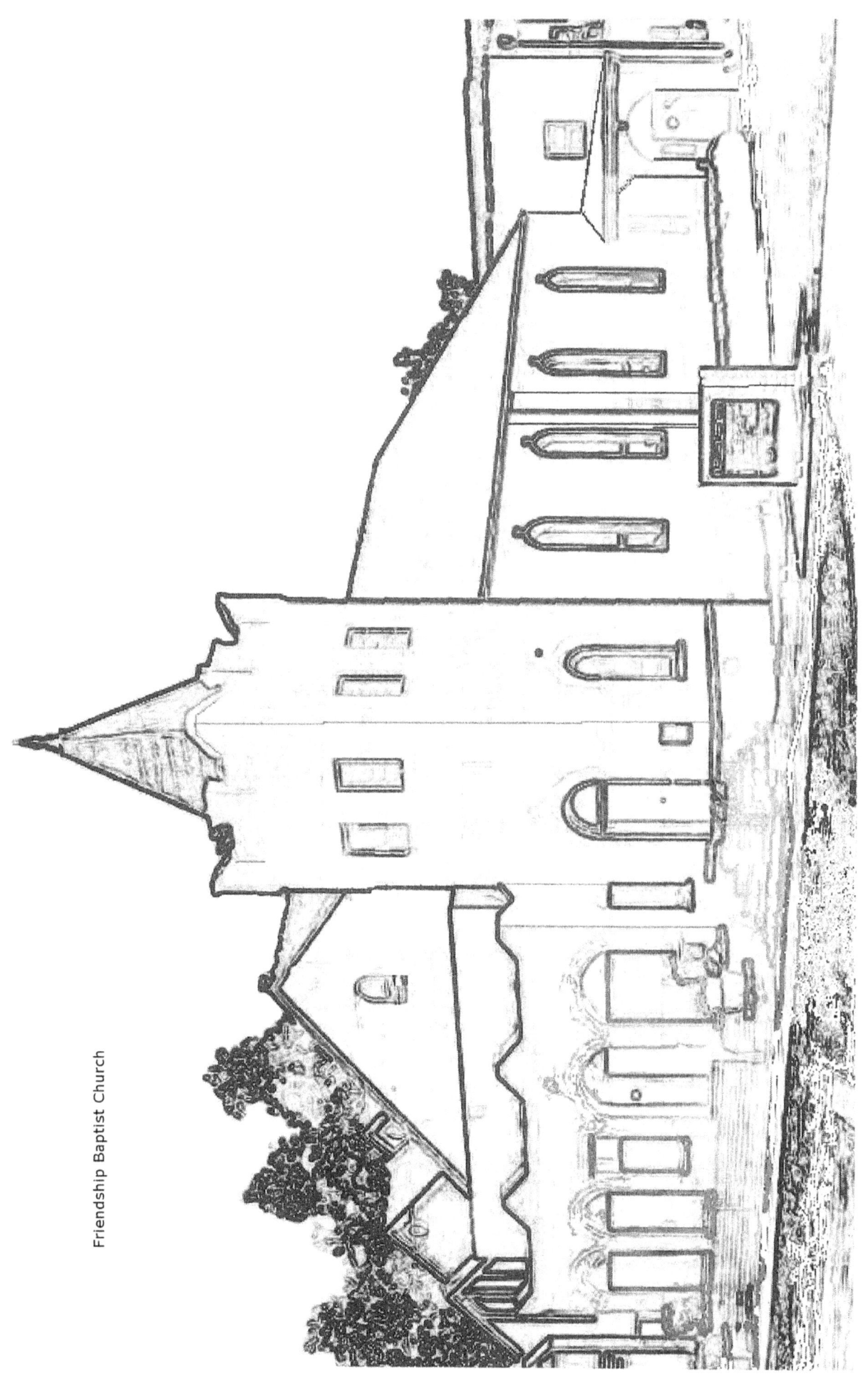

Friendship Baptist Church

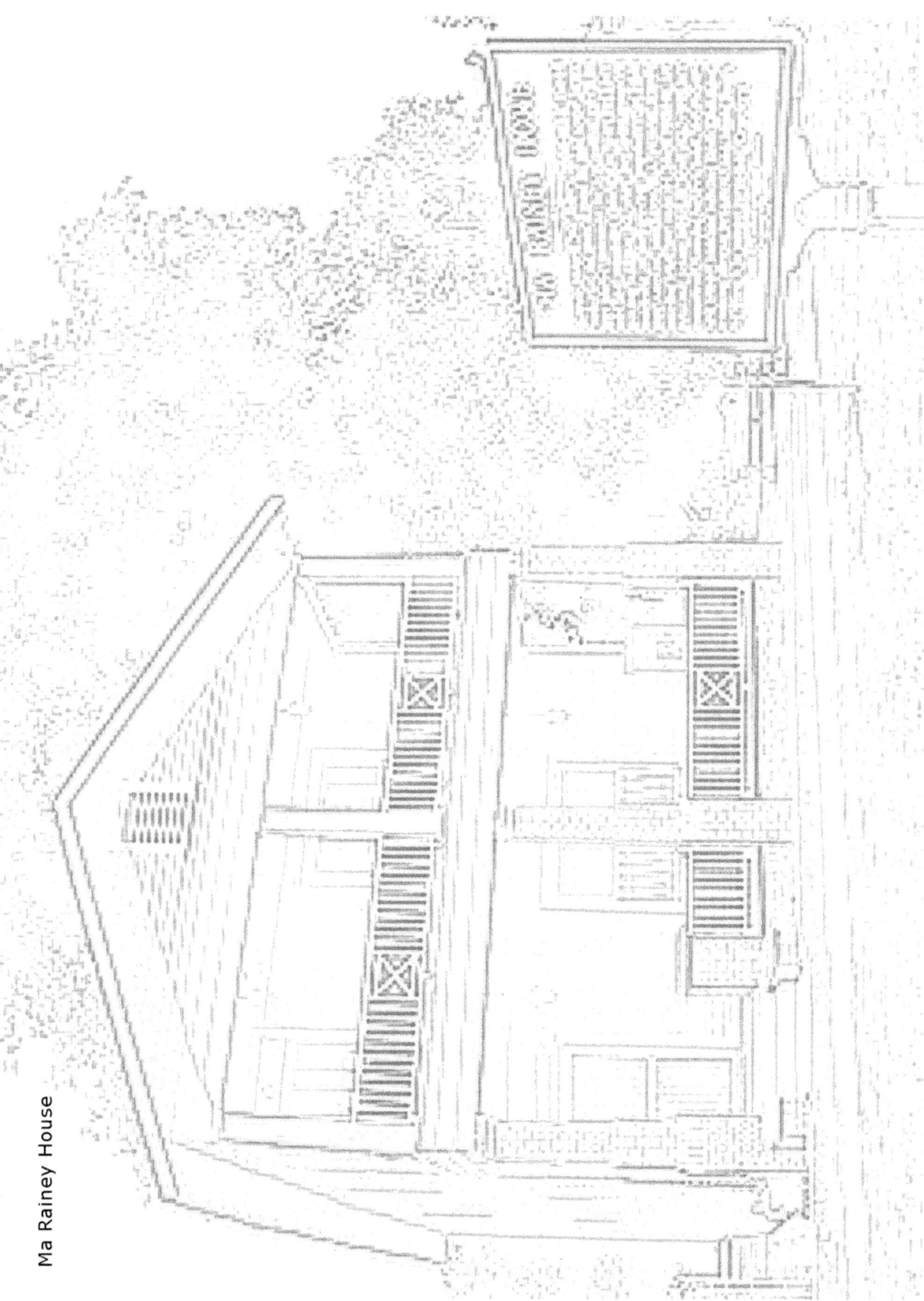

Ma Rainey House

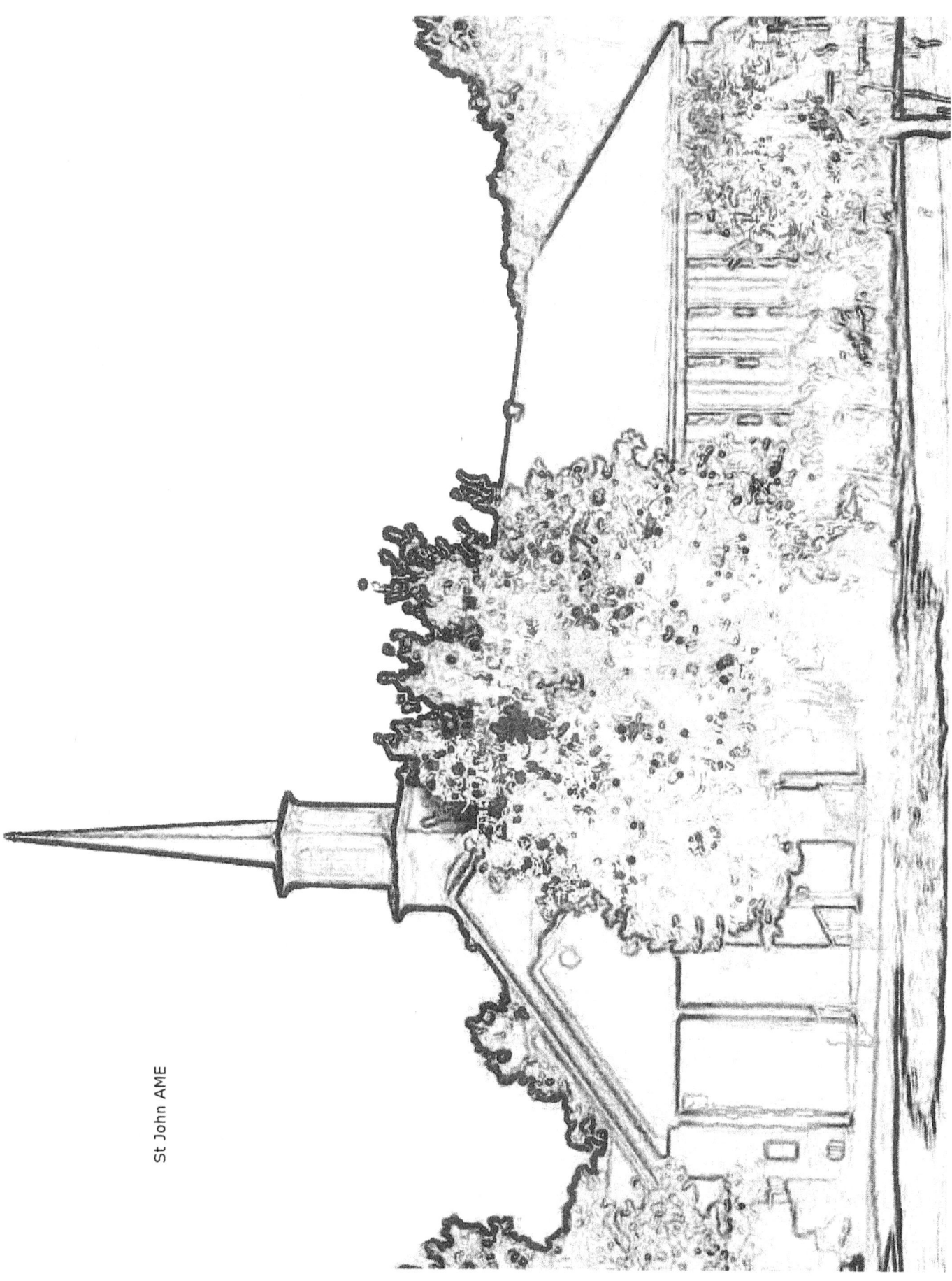

St John AME